POPULAR CULTURE

A VIEW FROM THE PAPARAZZI

Orlando Bloom

Kelly Clarkson

Johnny Depp

Hilary Duff

Will Ferrell

Jake Gyllenhaal

Paris and
Nicky Hilton

LeBron James

John Legend

Lindsay Lohan

Mandy Moore

Ashlee and
Jessica Simpson

Justin
Timberlake

Owen and
Luke Wilson

Tiger Woods

John Legend

Clara Magram

Mason Crest Publishers

John Legend

FRONTIS
Although John Legend's music career has only begun, the award-winning young singer and pianist is already living up to his name.

Produced by 21st Century Publishing and Communications, Inc.

MASON CREST PUBLISHERS INC.
370 Reed Road
Broomall, Pennsylvania 19008
(866) MCP-BOOK (toll free)
www.masoncrest.com

Printed in the United States.

First Printing

9 8 7 6 5 4 3 2 1

Magram, Clara.
    John Legend / Clara Magram.
        p. cm. — (Pop culture: a view from the paparazzi)
    Includes bibliographical references and index.
    Hardback edition: ISBN-13: 978-1-4222-0076-6
    Paperback edition: ISBN-13: 978-1-4222-0360-6
  1. Legend, John.   2. Rhythm and blues musician—United States—Biography.
I. Title.
ML420.L296M34 2008
782.421643092—dc22
[B]   2007020686

Publisher's notes:
  • All quotations in this book come from original sources, and contain the spelling and grammatical inconsistencies of the original text.

  • The Web sites mentioned in this book were active at the time of publication. The publisher is not responsible for Web sites that have changed their addresses or discontinued operation since the date of publication. The publisher will review and update the Web site addresses each time the book is reprinted.

CONTENTS

John Legend poses backstage with the three Grammy Awards he won in February 2006. Legend left the 48th annual Grammy Awards ceremony with the awards for Best New Artist, Best R&B Album (for his debut album *Get Lifted*), and Best Male R&B Vocal Performance (for his hit song "Ordinary People").

1

Stepping Into the Spotlight

Every year musicians and producers crowd into the Staples Center in downtown Los Angeles for the annual Grammy Awards ceremony. All are hoping to win one of the prestigious awards for musical excellence. Outside, fans scream with excitement and photographers scramble to take pictures. It is a night of talented stars, high fashion, and world-class entertainment.

The Grammy Awards, originally known as the Gramophone Awards, have been awarded every year since 1958. The judges include famous musicians who listen to hundreds of recordings, selecting winners from among the most outstanding performers and producers. The National Academy of Recording Arts and Sciences of the United States announces its lucky winners on the annual awards night. For all musicians, it is an honor just to be nominated for a Grammy Award. Winning a Grammy can help make a young artist into a star.

An Exciting Evening

The 48th annual Grammy Awards ceremony, which was held on the evening of February 8, 2006, was particularly exciting for 27-year-old singer/songwriter John Legend. He was scheduled to play the piano and sing his hit "Ordinary People" during the show, which would be seen by a live audience of about 20,000 people in the arena, as well as some 1.4 million television viewers.

But playing before this huge audience was not the most exciting part of the night. John had been nominated for eight Grammy Awards. His album *Get Lifted* had been nominated for Best **R&B** Album, while his hit single "Ordinary People" had received three nominations, for Song of the Year, Best R&B Song, and Best R&B Male Vocal Performance. Another song from *Get Lifted*, "Stay With You," was nominated for Best Traditional R&B Performance. John earned a nomination for Best R&B Performance by a Duo or Group for "So High," a song he recorded with singer Lauryn Hill. "They Say," a song he recorded with the rapper Common, was nominated for Best Rap/Sung Collaboration. Finally, he was nominated for Best New Artist.

In Ohio, where John's family lived, his relatives could scarcely believe the exciting news. John had been raised in Ohio, with his parents teaching him about music and supporting his performing interests from an early age. John had always felt confident about his ability as a musician, and knew that he had a creative spark. Now he was finally getting national recognition for his talent. He told a reporter about his mother's reaction to his Grammy nominations:

"My mom was screamin' 'Hallelujah!' She was very excited. Both of my parents are very proud—they always have been."

John Legend (third from left) poses with members of his family, including his father Ronald Stephens (left), his mother Phyllis Stephens (second from right), and several of his siblings at a party held after the 2007 Grammy Awards ceremony. John's family has always been supportive of his desire for a career in music.

Almost overnight, John had become a household name. His family watched in awe while John entered the awards ceremony to mingle with the top celebrities in American music.

John's Time to Shine

John seemed unusually calm as he walked across the red carpet into the bright lights of the lobby in the Staples Center. Smiling, the young singer told reporters:

"Whatever awards come, they come. It's going to be a fun night, either way."

John was no stranger to the buzz and the flashing lights of the Grammy Awards. In 2005 he sang onstage at the ceremony to accompany his friend, the acclaimed R&B singer Kanye West. John and Mavis Staples had performed "I'll Take You There," a song by The Staple Singers, in the midst of Kanye's hit "Jesus Walks." Kanye took center stage that night, going on to win three Grammys, but John knew his own time to shine was just around the corner. Shortly before the 2006 Grammy Awards ceremony, he recalled in an interview:

"People were telling me at the [2005] Grammys, like, 'John, you're going to be here next year, you're going to be doing well. . . . Everybody had a feeling that this could happen, but you never know the magnitude and I never expected it to be this big, the number of nominations."

John was one of several people who performed at the 2006 Grammys. Perhaps the most famous was former Beatle Paul McCartney, who had interrupted one of John's rehearsals to tell him that "Ordinary People" was a beautiful song. Other musicians who participated in the show included country singer Keith Urban, the band U2, Kelly Clarkson, Mary J. Blige, and Mariah Carey. John's friend Kanye West also performed at the Grammys. Among all these superstars, John held his own. When his turn came, he wowed the audience at the Staples Center.

The Triple Win

After John's stellar performance, there was one thing left to do that night: win some trophies. With nominations in eight categories, John had plenty of opportunities to do just that. When all the votes were counted, he had won three Grammy Awards: Best New Artist, Best R&B Album, and Best R&B Male Vocal Performance. John's smashing success at the Grammy Awards ceremony confirmed his belief that his career was heading in the right direction. In an interview with *The Orange County Register*, he revealed his deepest hope about the big win:

❝I think it validated me trusting my instincts as a creative person. It gave me more confidence and boldness to take creative risks on [the next] album.❞

When he left the Staples Center after the 2006 ceremony, John carried his three Grammys with pride. The trophies were small gold gramophones mounted on plaques bearing his name. It seemed that a legendary musical career was just beginning.

An excited John thanks the audience at the Staples Center in Los Angeles after receiving the award for Best Male R&B Vocal Performance at the 2006 Grammy ceremony. With John are members of the group Black Eyed Peas, who presented the award. Will.i.am (wearing hat) helped John write his award-winning song "Ordinary People."

Although he was born John Stephens, John eventually adopted "Legend" as his stage surname. "It was a nickname that started with a few friends," he explained in 2005. "They thought I sounded like I came from another era and had that old-school vibe. Eventually I adopted it. But it's not on my checks or anything."

2

Talent at an Early Age

John Legend was born John Stephens on December 28, 1978, in Springfield, Ohio. His father Ronald, a factory worker, and his mother Phyllis, a **seamstress**, encouraged their young son's interest in music. When John was just four years old, his grandmother began teaching him to play the piano. John especially loved **gospel music**, the spiritual harmonies of African-American churches.

Growing up in Springfield, John stood out from his friends and classmates. By the time he was 11 years old he was directing a local gospel choir, composing new

arrangements of songs and conducting the singers. "We grew up in church," he later told an interviewer:

> **"My grandmother was a church organist, my mother was a choir director, my dad was a drummer and a minister, my grandfather was a pastor. Most kids would have been forced to take piano lessons. I was like, 'Mom, I want to take lessons.'"**

While he was especially gifted in music, he was also a very good student and proved to be a leader as well. His classmates at Springfield North High School elected John president of the student body, vice president of the youth counsel, and king of the prom. He enjoyed singing in the school's show choir and performing onstage in the student theater. "I was always ambitious about everything," John said years later, looking back at his childhood in Springfield. "I would do everything at once."

His determination made him a real star in the classroom. John skipped several grades and finished high school early, graduating as **salutatorian** of his class. He later told an interviewer:

> **"I went to high school when I was 12 and I graduated when I was 16. They used to call me Doogie [after Doogie Howser, a television character who was a teenage doctor.] My saving grace was that I could sing. I killed [at] all the talent shows, but I was still a nerd."**

Off to College

Because of his good grades, John could choose where he wanted to go to college. The 16-year-old turned down offers from such renowned schools as Harvard and Georgetown. Instead, he decided to attend one of the country's best Ivy League schools, the University of Pennsylvania, which is located in downtown Philadelphia. John decided to major in English, taking many courses in African-American literature.

Years later, John explained why he decided to attend college, rather than seek a career in music right away. In 2005 he told a reporter for *Jet* magazine:

> **"**I figured [going to college] would give me more options if music didn't work out or if music was just something I did on the side. I didn't know what was going to happen. As I got further into school, I realized that I wanted to really make a career out of music.**"**

Because he was such a good student, John was able to earn good grades and still find time for his music. He joined a student group that sang **a cappella**, a popular style of singing without any instrumental accompaniment. In college, a cappella singers develop a sound that uses their vocal cords to produce appealing harmonies. The other members of Penn's college singing group, Counterparts, appreciated

Gospel music had a major influence on John, pictured here inside a church. "I've been in church choirs since I was, like, six, and I've been directing them since I was 10 or 11," he told *People* magazine in March 2005. "It influences the way I arrange music, the melodies I hear, the harmonies I hear."

John's talent, skill, musical knowledge, and creativity. John eventually became the group's arranger and producer.

To earn extra money, John worked at Bethel African Methodist Episcopal Church in Scranton, a community 90 miles north of Philadelphia.

John started playing the piano when he was very young. By the time he went to college in Philadelphia he was an accomplished pianist. While attending the University of Pennsylvania, one of the oldest universities in the United States, John directed the school's a cappella group Counterparts. The coed singing group performs jazz and pop tunes.

He juggled several roles at the church: pianist, choir director, and head of the music department. In his free time, he performed his own music at local nightclubs, singing and playing the piano.

John's First Recording Job

While he was a student at the University of Pennsylvania, John made some important new friends in the music industry. When he was 19 years old, a friend named Tara Michel introduced John to Lauryn Hill, a singer who had become famous with a group called The Fugees. Tara had agreed to sing background vocals on a solo album that Lauryn was working on titled *The Miseducation of Lauryn Hill*. She told Lauryn to listen to John play the piano. John impressed Lauryn so much that she offered him a job playing on one of her songs, "Everything is Everything." John later recalled:

> **"I didn't know if it was guaranteed that she was going to use what I did. Finally when the record came out and I saw my name on there, I was ecstatic. Nice bragging rights at school when everyone's listening to the Lauryn Hill album and you're able to say you're on it."**

It seemed that everyone was listening to *The Miseducation of Lauryn Hill* after the album was released in 1998. It sold more than 400,000 copies in its first week and topped the *Billboard* R&B Album charts for six weeks.

Lauryn Hill later invited John to audition to become a member of her band. "I tried out but didn't make it," John said. "I was all ready to quit college and go on tour."

The Young Business Professional

In 1999 John graduated **magna cum laude** from the University of Pennsylvania. His academic record made him an attractive candidate for jobs all over the country. Prestigious companies wanted to hire him right after college. The 20-year-old soon got a job at Boston Consulting Group, a firm that helps businesses develop financial strategies. For John, this was the next big chapter in his life: moving to New York to start a business career in corporate America.

John had never expected to end up as a business consultant. He still believed that his career would be in music. A few years later, after

When former Fugees singer Lauryn Hill heard John play piano, she invited the then-unknown musician to play on her song "Everything Is Everything." John was thrilled when he learned the song had been included on the biggest-selling album of 1998, the critically acclaimed *Miseducation of Lauryn Hill*. The album was nominated for 11 Grammy Awards and won five.

Get Lifted was released, John told *Interview* magazine how he felt shortly after finishing college:

"When I was younger I thought I was supposed to have a record deal by age 19 or 20. When it didn't happen, I would get frustrated, but I would keep working and progressing and making new songs and recording new demos. And I kept thinking these people are stupid, they should've signed me a long time ago."

However, having a full-time job had important benefits—particularly the salary of about $50,000 a year. "I needed money. I lived in New York and had to pay my rent," John told the *Washington Post*. For the next few years, John spent his days working at a desk in the offices of Boston Consulting Group. In the evenings, he returned to the music world to play for modest crowds in small New York nightclubs.

Taking the First Steps

In 2000, John released his first album of original music, which was titled *John Stephens*. It was an **amateur** CD he had recorded and produced entirely by himself. John described the early recording:

> **"It was almost like a research project where you market-test your music with the fans and see what they like the most, what they respond to the most. It helps you home in on what you want to go out with."**

Over the next few years John put out three more CDs, each of which was a recording of his live performances. His fans responded with enthusiastic praise. People who liked John's music bought his CDs at his shows and online at his personal Web site.

Taking a Stage Name

Around this time the young musician adopted the name that he now uses professionally. A friend had nicknamed him "John Legend" because of the classic sound of his music. He later told the London *Sunday Times*:

> **"A guy came in when we were recording, and he was like, 'Man, you sound like you came from another era; like a throwback to Stevie Wonder, Marvin Gaye. We should just call you The Legend.' And I was like, 'Yeah, ha, ha.' Then everyone in the room's going 'Yeah, John Legend, that's hot.' . . . I thought that was the end of it. But then they would introduce me as that, so it became my de facto new stage name."**

John was aware that people might hear the name and think he was boastful or cocky. But he also knew the positive word "legend" would give him something to aim for in his music career. He told the *Sunday Times*:

❝I felt it might give me some negative attention, but I figured if people pay me any attention, well, I'll just have to convince them with my music.❞

The Birth of a Musical Partnership

John's former roommate at the University of Pennsylvania, DeVon Harris, provided him with a valuable link to the music industry. DeVon, who changed his name to Devo Springsteen, was a disc jockey who shared John's passion for music. Devo had a cousin who was an up-and-coming music producer from Chicago named Kanye West. In 2001, a few months after graduating from Penn, Devo brought his cousin to see John perform at a nightclub.

Meeting Kanye West proved to be a turning point in John's career, as the two musicians developed a strong bond. In 2005 Kanye told *Essence* magazine, "If we were both 12-year-olds and doing a talent show for our parents, they'd probably say, 'Well, I don't know about Kanye, but that John Legend is a talented boy!'"

Kanye saw star material in John, who was then just 22 years old. By the next day, John was jamming in a recording studio as Kanye listened. A musical partnership was born. John teamed up with Kanye to appear as a **session musician** on albums by Mary J. Blige, the rapper Common, Talib Kweli, the Black Eyed Peas, Slum Village, Janet Jackson, and Dilated Peoples. He sang on a song by Alicia Keys, "You Don't Know My Name," and appeared on Jay-Z's acclaimed *Black Album*. John later said:

> **"Clearly, it gave me a lot of experience working with great artists on classic albums. Anytime you get that kind of experience, it will rub off on you. So I learned to make the best of those opportunities, and it helped me to make my project [his own music] better."**

John continued looking for a record label in the hope of making a professional album of his own. But the big companies had never heard of him, and they were not interested. John remained hopeful about his music, thanks to the support of his fans. He later told a reporter at the *Washington Post*:

> **"Even though the industry wasn't responding to it as much as I wanted them to, I had fans in every city on the East Coast who were really into it, and I was selling a lot of CDs on my Web site. I figured I need to make the rest of the world hear it like these guys are hearing it and eventually it will take off."**

Kanye had ambitions of his own, both as a producer and as a hip-hop artist. When he put out his debut album in 2004, *The College Dropout*, he hired John to play piano and sing on the recording. The album was a smash hit and Kanye picked up 10 Grammy nominations in 2005. John's contributions to the recording did not go unnoticed. Some music executives were beginning to see his potential.

Kanye West (right) and John Legend pose for photos at the 2005 MTV Video Music Awards ceremony in Miami. John helped Kanye write several songs on his award-winning album *The College Dropout*, and also sang and played piano on several tracks, including the hit single "Jesus Walks," which reached number two on Billboard's Hot R&B/Hip Hop Singles chart.

3

Touring Toward Fame

For Kanye West 2004 was a great year. Just a year older than John, he was skyrocketing to stardom thanks to the success of his album. Throughout the United States and Europe people watched Kanye's music videos and listened to his CDs. Kanye's phenomenal popularity would bring new attention to John Legend's own talents.

Kanye had been born in Atlanta, although he grew up in Chicago. Like John he came from a comfortable, middle-class family; his mother was an English professor at Chicago State University. Kanye entered college in Chicago but soon dropped out to pursue his passion for music. Fans came to know him as a producer, a musical innovator, an outspoken political commentator, and even a fashion columnist for *Complex* magazine.

The release of *The College Dropout* made Kanye a huge star. Fans saw him interviewed on Black Entertainment Television (BET) and watched him perform on MTV. He even appeared on the prestigious BBC music show *Top of the Pops*. These appearances helped worldwide sales of his album top 2 million copies.

On the Road With Superstars

John appreciated his relationship with the superstar singer. He would later tell *People* how Kanye helped him to develop and improve his sound:

> **"He has great instincts. He gives me a lot of good advice on a creative level. We critique each other's songs, productions. He also gives me good advice on dealing with the record industry."**

In early 2004 Kanye asked John to join him on a performance tour that would crisscross the United States. John agreed to play backup for Kanye in cities around the country, including Chicago and Washington, D.C. The two friends went their separate ways after that, with Kanye touring in England, Holland, and Germany while John went back to playing smaller clubs in the United States.

That August Kanye and John were both invited to join another performer's national tour. In the summer of 2004 27-year-old Usher was the most popular R&B artist in the United States. In a single week, three of his songs appeared among the top 10 singles on *Billboard* magazine music chart. Only two other music groups, the Beatles and the Bee Gees, had previously accomplished this feat. His album *Confessions* set an R&B record by selling 1.1 million copies in the United States in its first week. Usher's singing style was young and hip, and the fans loved it.

Usher had scheduled six weeks of performances on huge stages in 24 American cities. Music fans rushed to get tickets for his "Truth Tour." During a fast-paced summer of traveling and performing, John collaborated with Kanye and Usher and shared their spotlight.

A New Challenge

Doing national tours with professional musicians was the opportunity of a lifetime for 25-year-old John Legend. The tour exposed his talent

"He has great instincts," John told *People* magazine about his mentor Kanye West, who is pictured here during a performance. "He gives me a lot of good advice on a creative level. We critique each other's songs, productions. He also gives me good advice on dealing with the record industry."

Although John was only a supporting performer when he toured with R&B superstar Usher in 2004, he did attract some attention. When Neil Drumming of Entertainment Weekly reviewed a performance on Usher's Truth Tour in Virginia, he called John a "charismatic singer-keyboardist," and suggested that he deserved a bigger part in the show.

Performing before huge stadium crowds presented a different challenge for John, as he was used to playing for much smaller crowds in nightclubs. However, his successful high-profile performances enabled John to take the next step in his musical career. Impressed by his talent, Columbia Records signed him to a recording contract.

to thousands of new people, and John gained a great deal of experience as a performer. Every night he had an opportunity to play in front of enormous crowds of people.

The Truth Tour concerts were very different than the small-venue **gigs** that John was used to playing. In the bars and nightclubs where he used to sing and play piano John could respond to the moods of listeners and watch them soak in his music. But in the larger stadiums he was far from the listeners, and could barely make out the faces of people in the audience. However, playing in front of the massive, cheering crowds did not bother John at all. In an interview with *MTV News* in 2004, he explained:

> **❝There is no pressure because they are not there to see me—my name is not on the bill. I am just an added treat.❞**

All the attention forced the music industry to finally open its doors to John. In May 2004 he got a recording contract with Columbia Records. His career seemed to be taking off.

An Album of His Own

Not only did Kanye West agree to produce John's debut album, he also offered to release it on his new record label, G.O.O.D. (Getting Out Our Dreams) Music, which was affiliated with Columbia. Kanye provided rhythm tracks for many of the songs on John's album, which would be titled *Get Lifted*. John's friend Devo Springsteen also helped with the album's production.

Perhaps John's most unusual collaborator on *Get Lifted* was the rapper Snoop Dogg, who was featured on the song "I Can Change." Snoop is notorious for **gangsta rap** songs that glorify violence and drug use, but John liked the rapper's rhythmic vocal style. In "I Can Change" Snoop's singing is combined with spiritual music and a gospel choir backs up the track. In an article on his Web site, John described his style:

> **❝It's very soulful, rooted in gospel but with hip-hop beats and unique, witty lyrics . . . more of a 'feel good,' upbeat sound.❞**

Get Lifted was the first album released under Kanye's G.O.O.D. Music label. It hit store shelves on December 28, 2004—John's 26th birthday. John was hoping for the best. His **savvy** production team and talented backup musicians had put in hours of hard work on the debut album. Now all that mattered was whether consumers would like the music. John's optimism shone through in an interview with *JET* magazine:

> **❝I feel like this album is one of those albums that'll get good word of mouth. Just put it in people's hands and it'll sell itself. It all comes down to making good songs.❞**

Good songs certainly do sell albums, but nobody could have predicted the level of success that John's debut achieved. The world reacted to *Get Lifted* in a way that surprised everyone, exceeding even the expectations of the album's confident creator.

Topping the Charts

Get Lifted was an instant success. The album's first single, "Used to Love U," was a minor hit on the U.S. R&B/Hip-Hop chart. *Get Lifted* debuted

John takes a break in the recording studio. Kanye West helped produce his debut album, *Get Lifted*, and he contributed vocals to John's song "Number One." Others who collaborated on John's debut included rapper Snoop Dogg, singer Lauryn Hill, violinist Miri Ben-Ari, and members of John's family, who sang on the track "It Don't Have to Change."

at number seven on the *Billboard* Top 200 chart of albums, and at number one on the R&B Album chart.

Music critics loved the album. They felt that John's earnest, sentimental melodies stood apart from the modern trend of blending hip-hop into R&B songs. *Time* commented, "Singer John Legend . . . shows he's on his way to living up to his presumptuous stage name with *Get Lifted*, his assured, accomplished debut album." *Newsweek*

The cover of *Get Lifted*, which was released on John's birthday in 2004. Reviews of the record were uniformly positive. "This neo-soul newcomer (and Kanye West protégé) soars on an album that brings to mind such bona fide soul legends as Stevie Wonder, Donny Hathaway, and Al Green," noted *People* magazine.

magazine called John "soul's hottest new sensation" and said that *Get Lifted* "is one of those rare CDs that will really get you off the ground." The *Village Voice* named it one of the best albums of the year, based on a survey of hundreds of music critics.

In a review in *Entertainment Weekly*, Tom Sinclair compared John to Stevie Wonder, Smokey Robinson, Marvin Gaye, and other great R&B singers, writing:

> **"Like Ray Charles, Legend joins the spiritual and the secular in satisfying, sexy ways. . . . Almost every tune seduces with catchy hooks and soulful singing. . . . He may hang with hip-hoppers, but Legend knows good singing and good playing are what ordinary people want most."**

The public also showed that it appreciated John's talent, as fans bought the album in droves. *Get Lifted* eventually sold more than 1.5 million copies in the United States and over 3 million worldwide. John even got a personal call from talk-show host Oprah Winfrey, who voiced her enthusiastic approval for *Get Lifted*.

The praise for *Get Lifted* left John feeling somewhat stunned. He confessed to a *Washington Post* reporter:

> **"It's kind of crazy to me that so many people enjoy it. I can't really explain it. It's cool when people say they like it, but I'm already thinking about the next album and how much better I can make it."**

A Major Hit

Much of the praise for *Get Lifted* focused on the album's second single, "Ordinary People." John had originally written the song for an album by the group Black Eyed Peas together with band member will.i.am. In an interview with *MTV* News in 2004, John described how the song came into existence:

> **"Will played this hip-hop beat with these chords, and I just started singing the hook, 'We are ordinary people.' It just wasn't a Black Eyed Peas kind of song, so he let me use it for my album."**

John made the right decision by including "Ordinary People" on *Get Lifted*. The song reached number four on the U.S. R&B/Hip-Hop chart, and won a Grammy for Best R&B Male Vocal Performance in 2006.

"Ordinary People" displayed a range of John's talents. On the album, listeners could hear him singing and playing the piano, accompanied by an orchestra and harmonica. The song's lyrics described the struggles of people having arguments in their romantic relationships. With his rich, soulful voice, John reminded couples to "take it slow" in order to stay together:

"Ordinary People" is a simple but emotionally powerful song in which John sings about the difficulty that most people experience in romantic relationships. His piano playing provides the only instrumentation other than John's voice. The song was the biggest hit from *Get Lifted*, and won John a Grammy Award in 2006.

> " I know I misbehaved
> And you made your mistakes
> And we both got room left to grow
> And though love sometimes hurts
> I still put you first
> And we'll make this thing work
> But I think we should take it slow. "

Help from Family and Friends

John knew a little something about romantic conflicts. The lyrics of "Ordinary People" were inspired by a very special couple: his parents, who had divorced but remarried 12 years later. John's family also played a key role on another song from the album, "It Don't Have to Change." On this track, John and 15 members of his extended family sang about the importance of their relationships with each other. John described it to an *Interview* reporter:

> "That's my whole family in the background and on some of the leads as well—my uncles, my dad, my brothers, my sister, my mother, my aunts, my grandmother, and my cousins."

John's talented family also accompanied him to some of his concerts, where they joined him in singing onstage. Among them was his younger brother, Vaughn Anthony, who has followed in John's footsteps and become a professional R&B singer.

But the most important influence on the album was John's good friend Kanye West. John knew that without Kanye's endorsement, record companies might never have given him a chance. In 2006 he told the Associated Press:

> "People cared more about [*Get Lifted*] because [Kanye] was attached to it and he was an 'it' artist at the time and still is, even more so now. So it got more attention than just the average R&B singer would have got."

"I'm a product of my environment," John says about his musical style, which blends R&B, hip-hop, and gospel influences. "I grew up in church, but I also grew up listening to classic soul, R&B, gospel, and hip-hop. You can hear it in the music. . . . My role models are Stevie Wonder and Marvin Gaye."

4

High-Class Performances

With *Get Lifted* topping the charts, everyone in the music industry knew John Legend's name. Suddenly, the former session musician was in great demand. For the first time John had plenty of money. "When I got my first big check, I paid [my college loans] off. No more debt!" he told *People*:

"I bought a place [in Manhattan]. I just bought some art—some abstract stuff—and some collages are coming too. A friend who works at MoMA [the Museum of Modern Art

Entertainment producers from New York to Hollywood were calling John regularly with offers. John sang Stevie Wonder's song "Don't You Worry 'Bout a Thing" for the soundtrack of the Will Smith movie *Hitch*, which was released in 2005. A month later, he played Stevie Wonder in the television drama *American Dreams*, singing "Uptight (Everything's Alright)."

Being linked to Stevie Wonder, a singer who has sold more than 100 million album and won 22 Grammys, was very exciting for John.

Music legend Stevie Wonder (2nd from left) sings with John Legend (second from right) and other performers during a concert before Super Bowl XL in February 2006. Stevie Wonder is one of John's favorite performers, particularly for his albums *Talking Book* and *Music of My Mind*. John explains, "The songs— the way he was singing and writing—were just perfect."

He readily admits that he considers the Motown legend one of his greatest influences. In early 2005 he told *People*:

> **"Stevie [Wonder] is probably my favorite [soul legend] because he wrote and produced whole albums by himself. He's just extremely talented and made such beautiful albums in succession in the late '60s and early '70s."**

John teamed up with the real Stevie Wonder at the 2005 BET Awards in June, where they played a piano duet together. As if performing with a musical legend were not enough, the award show honored John even further that night, naming him Best New Artist. It was one of many awards he would win in the coming months.

Vocal Changes

In the summer of 2005, while John was touring with Alicia Keys, he had an unpleasant experience. During some performances the singer found himself short of breath and struggling to sing his songs. "My voice was *hurting*," he later explained. "I had to [get a vocal coach] because I'd never sung so much in my life."

The coach helped John learn how to breathe more effectively when he was singing. He also taught the singer to pace himself on stage, in order to save his voice. Part of the healing process meant that John had to give his strained vocal cords a break. For two weeks he tried to stop talking completely. He stayed out of the public eye and typed messages to friends on a computer keyboard in order to communicate. He commented:

> **"I didn't want to do that out in public. People would have been like, 'Why is John Legend typing?'"**

With proper breathing and a better vocal technique, John's voice came back stronger than ever. Soon, he could sing comfortably in the recording studio and on stage. He explained his recovery in an interview with *Entertainment Weekly*:

> **"My tone got smoother and cleaner. That's why I sound so different on my new album. I didn't plan to [change my style]. I had to switch it up."**

In 2005 John was invited to tour with R&B singer Alicia Keys; with them in this picture is actor Terrence Howard (left). Keys is an acclaimed singer/songwriter who has won nine Grammy Awards and sold 28 million albums in her career. During the tour John found that the stress of constant performing was taking a toll on his voice.

Helping the Less Fortunate

As he emerged as a star, John was willing to lend his talent to fund-raisers for important causes across the country. On April 11, 2005, he performed at the Beacon Theater in New York City to raise money for a cause he believed in: music education in America's public schools. The concert was part of a fundraiser for VH1 Save the Music, a foundation created in 1997 to support music education in public schools. In its first ten years, VH1 Save the Music donated $34 million worth of new musical instruments to schools.

On March 15, 2006, John joined a star-studded lineup of musicians in the grand ballroom of New York's Waldorf Astoria Hotel for "Hollywood Meets Motown," a benefit to support the National

John arrives at the VH1 Save the Music benefit concert in New York, April 2005. He performed his hit "Ordinary People" at the show, which was intended to raise money for music education in public schools. John also sang "Tell Me Something Good" with Joss Stone, and joined Rod Stewart and others on a rendition of "Stay With Me."

Colorectal Cancer Research Alliance. In addition to singing at the benefit, he also posed for photos with other celebrities, including R&B legend Smokey Robinson, singer/songwriter James Taylor, stylish jazz trumpeter Chris Botti, rapper Ludacris, television newscaster Katie Couric, and *Sesame Street* character Elmo.

A month later, John was in Los Angeles for the launch of "JC Penney Jam . . . The Concert for America's Kids." He attended a press conference at L.A.'s Shrine Auditorium on June 13, 2006, and performed the next day at a concert featuring rock musician Jon Bon Jovi, country musician Kenny Chesney, opera singer Andrea Bocelli, and other music stars. The program raised money to support after-school programs for children.

That month John also performed at a jazz fundraiser in New York with legendary jazz trumpeter Wynton Marsalis, the musical director of Jazz at Lincoln Center. "Mr. Marsalis is a genius," he proclaimed on his Web site after the show.

Applause and Awards

John was making a name for himself as a performer. In early February 2006 he was asked to be part of the Super Bowl's pregame show. Later that month he came to the Grammy Awards in Los Angeles with high hopes. He was nominated for eight awards, and came home with three Grammys, including Best New Artist. With an onstage performance of "Ordinary People," he dazzled the TV audience of nearly 1.4 million.

The Grammys were just one highlight in a year of honors for John. At the Soul Train Music Awards in March 2006, *Get Lifted* won the award for Best R&B/Soul Album, while "Ordinary People" was named Best R&B/Soul Single.

During the spring and summer after his first Grammy Awards success, John maintained a rigorous performing schedule. He teamed up with classic pop and jazz crooner Tony Bennett for Bennett's album and a related television special. He sang at the NBA All-Star Game's halftime show and during the seventh-inning stretch at Major League Baseball's All-Star Game. He even appeared on the children's television program *Sesame Street*, singing a duet with Hoots the Owl.

Working Toward a New Album

Despite his quiet, soulful **demeanor**, John actually enjoyed the excitement and challenges of performing. He got a thrill out of the enthusiastic crowds who came to hear him. When his music affected listeners' emotions, he felt deeply rewarded. In 2005, he told a reporter for *Grammys* magazine:

> **"I feel like my shows are a combination of a revival to some extent—it's kind of spiritual. People go away and feel touched and energized."**

John was growing as a professional singer, and he changed more than his singing style. The success of *Get Lifted* helped John to trust his musical instincts, to follow wherever his creativity led. For his next project, he decided to branch off in a new direction. John wrote different types of songs, trusting that his loyal fans would stick with him through the change.

"It's so exciting. There are so many things happening every day," John told *Ebony* magazine when asked about his career. **"I'm working hard every day and getting more recognition. Crowds know who I am. I was used to having to win them over. But now, they know the music already. They are excited to see me."**

In addition to touring to support his album *Get Lifted*, in 2006 John appeared at a number of high-profile sporting events. These included an appearance at a Super Bowl pregame concert, a performance at the NBA All-Star Game's halftime show, and singing "God Bless America" during the seventh-inning stretch at Major League Baseball's All-Star Game.

John poses for a photo with several female fans. "I'm single with no children, and there are more women—definitely more women," the sexy bachelor told *Ebony* magazine in April 2005. "There are a lot of beautiful women out there, but it can be dangerous if you approach [the situation] with reckless abandon."

Like a typical music fan, John spends much of his free time listening to a variety of music on the radio, television, and on recorded albums. Turning the radio dial brings up R&B, soul, Motown, rap, hip hop, alternative rock, and other styles. His own musical taste has continued to evolve as he hears more of the world's different sounds. In an interview with the *Washington Post*, he described his transformation:

"I'm ahead of where I was in my songwriting, production, even my singing. I've learned more about my voice and what I want to do with it. I also want to make the arrangements more dynamic and fluid."

Verizon Wireless
CONNECT
FALL 2006

new this issue:
make your phone your own
with music, tones, accessories, and more!

plus:
stay **in** touch with the
AMERICA'S CHOICE®
FAMILY SHAREPLAN

get **JOHN LEGEND's** number

"I'm really kind of shy and laid-back," John Legend admitted to *People* magazine in 2006. "[But] I've always been very at ease onstage." Since emerging as a major star on the R&B music scene with the release of *Get Lifted*, John has been pictured on the covers of many magazines.

5

The Evolving Artist

Just as he predicted, John came out with an entirely different brand of music for his second album, *Once Again*. Music reviewers described it as more soulful than the R&B, hip-hop mix of *Get Lifted*. The British newspaper *The Guardian* praised *Once Again* by comparing it to the work of other legendary musicians:

> "His tunes are little Motown-ish symphonies, lit from within by his quiet-storm intensity, itself beholden to Smokey Robinson."

New Directions

With *Once Again*, John drew on inspirations different from those that had motivated him for *Get Lifted*. The album featured warmer, more emotional tones. His thoughts had turned to love, he told a reporter at the *Orange County Register*:

> **"I didn't plan to make this album less hip-hop, but my writing and production started to lean in a more soulful, romantic direction this time."**

John was now older and more mature, and with his new album he was ready to tackle serious topics: long-term love, loss, and even death. In "Coming Home," he sang about a soldier missing his family and worrying that he might die in battle. Songs like "Where Did My Baby Go" evoke the pain of losing a loved one. On John's MySpace page he discussed the way that "Where Did My Baby Go" evolved and fit into *Once Again*:

> **"It was one of the only songs written before I began recording this album, and was in my head for a long time. I didn't know what I was going to do with it because at the time it didn't sound like anything I'd done before. It ended up fitting perfectly because I ended up writing more stuff in that direction so it became a precursor to where I was going this time."**

As John forged a new path with his music, he continued to work with his friend and producer Kanye West. Kanye produced the album's second single "Heaven" and contributed masterful backup vocals. Others who contributed to *Once Again* included old friends will.i.am and Devo Springsteen, as well as Raphael Saadiq, Craig Street, Sa-Ra, Eric Hudson, Dave Tozer, and the production team Avenue.

Trying Different Things

John and will.i.am co-produced the album's first single, "Save Room." The song is unusual because unlike most of John's songs, it does not feature his piano playing. This allows John to show off his ability as a vocalist. The song samples from "Stormy," a hit tune of the 1960s. "Will.i.am brought the sample," John later explained:

> **"I didn't even know the original. I just knew it was a nice organ sound and wanted to write to it. I just started mumbling along to it, finding my place in the melody and it worked for me."**

In the future John may do more music that does not center around his piano playing. He has even told interviewers that he has considered taking up a new instrument, the guitar, because musical technique

John Legend works with technicians in the recording studio while making his second album, *Once Again*. "I knew [making this album] would be a challenge," Legend said, "but if it helps me be known for putting out distinct cool music rather than following the trends, that's a better position for me to be in."

always came easily to him and he had already mastered piano and vocal performances. He told a *USA Today* reporter:

> **That's one of those New Year's resolutions that you never get done. [But] it would give me more ideas. You write differently depending on the instrument. A guitar is more portable and more earthly in some ways, and it might inspire me to go in different directions.**

A Great Response

The new album was another success, debuting at number three on the Billboard 200 chart and at number one on the R&B Album chart. *Once Again* sold 231,000 copies in the U.S. in its first week, more than double the opening sales of *Get Lifted*. It went on to sell more than a million copies and was certified **platinum** in the United States.

As had been the case with *Get Lifted*, music critics loved *Once Again*. *People's* Chuck Arnold wrote, "*Once Again* finds Legend taking it up a notch from *Get Lifted*," while *Rolling Stone's* Jonathan Ringen called *Once Again* the "bigger, better follow-up" to John's debut album. Cary Darling of the *Fort Worth Star-Telegram* wrote:

> **Minimalist and acoustic in tone if not in actual execution, *Once Again* is a sweetly triumphant throwback to the days of traditional R&B. . . . In an era of feverish over-production and "American Idol"-style vocal bombast, Legend's low-key yet heart-felt humanity and creative classicism are especially rewarding. . . . [*Once Again* is] one of the best albums of the year.**

Another good review appeared in the influential publication *All Music Guide*, where Andy Kellman wrote:

> **Once Again is much more focused than *Get Lifted*, and the quality of its songs is equally high. . . . It's more assured and sounds nothing like an experiment to see what sticks. Legend now knows exactly where he fits, and he's not holding back in the least.**

"We made these songs in the studio and we thought they might work, but it's really validating when you can bring them to life and see how the crowd reacts to them," John said after the release of *Once Again*. "To do that every night . . . is very uplifting. I'm genuinely happier because I'm able to do this."

Music insiders liked the album as well. John picked up three more Grammy nominations and was invited back to play onstage at the ceremony in Los Angeles for the second year in a row.

Another Round of Grammy Wins

At the 2007 Grammys, John performed with two other singers, Corinne Bailey Rae and John Mayer. Each artist played his or her own composition, accompanied by the other two. When it was John's turn, he sang "Coming Home" from *Once Again*.

John left at the end of the night with more than just another success-ful performance under his belt. The judges sent him home that night with two more Grammy Awards: one for Best R&B Male Vocal Performance for his song "Heaven," and another award for Best R&B Performance By a Duo or Group With Vocals for his song "Family Affair."

On his Web site, John expressed thanks to his fans worldwide. He wrote about the tremendous effect of fame on his creativity and ambition:

John meets the Dixie Chicks—Emily Robison, Natalie Maines, and Marty Maguire—at a party after the 2007 Grammy Awards ceremony. The ceremony marked another milestone in John's career. He performed at the show for the second year in a row, and two of his songs from *Once Again* won Grammys.

"To have the chance to see your music be elevated and to have almost universally positive response to that music makes me feel better every day. I feel more confident and inspired, and that's fun. I'm feeling truly creative and I'm hoping that feeling will stay around, because my hope and belief is that most people are down to grow and explore with me."

Back on the Road

After the release of *Once Again,* John crisscrossed the globe on a world tour. He performed in nightclubs and stadiums. As an American performer, he represented the United States to the foreign countries where he traveled. Some of his fans overseas could not speak English. Even though they did not understand the words, they loved the depth and feeling of John's music.

Traveling helped John to develop his own sense of connection to fellow Americans and his interest in world events. He became increasingly involved in social activism. After Hurricane Katrina devastated communities along the Gulf coast such as New Orleans in the summer of 2005, John heard about the difficulties that faced the millions of people who had lost their homes in the storm. He has joined other compassionate entertainers in playing at fundraisers to raise money for the hurricane's victims.

John often has very strong views about politics and sometimes expresses his thoughts on his Web site. Until now, he has kept his views separate from his music. But if inspiration strikes, he may one day use his music to call for social change. In 2006, he told the *Washington Post*:

"The social stuff is heavy on my mind right now, so I'm sure it will creep into my songwriting. But I'll write whatever comes."

Other Projects

In addition to promoting his own albums and writing new songs, John keeps busy with a variety of projects. He assisted Kanye West on his forthcoming album *Graduation,* which is scheduled for release in 2007, and he has also worked on albums for some other G.O.O.D. Music artists, including the rapper Common and the hip-hop ensemble Fort

Minor. He also contributed to the song "Please Baby Don't" on Sergio Mendes's album *Timeless*.

According to some reports, John is even helping pop superstar Michael Jackson with his next album. If these rumors are true, the collaboration would be quite a thrill for John. In interviews, he has credited Jackson with helping to inspire his own career when he was young. "I used to watch Michael Jackson on television," he said. "I figured I could do what he was doing."

John made a brief foray into acting with his small role as Stevie Wonder on *American Dreams*. He looked to expand on that experience when he joined the cast of *Stringbean & Marcus*, a feature film starring hip-hop performer Mos Def and actress Sophie Okonedo. The movie, which is scheduled for release in 2007, focuses on a broken love affair between two former members of the **Black Panthers**. The movie is set in Philadelphia. John vowed to give the production his full attention during the filming process:

> **"It should be cool. I don't know how long my acting career will go and if I'm going to really focus on it or not, but I'm going to really focus on getting that role right and if I do well with that, then I'll continue."**

Musical Inspirations and Influences

John has come a long way since his gospel choir performances as a boy growing up in Ohio. He no longer attends church every week, but religion continues to influence his life. In 2004, he told the Web site JustJared.com:

> **"My musical background is gospel music, so that's where I grew up playing. So I think that influences everything that I do because whatever you grow up learning is the core of what you do musically. And so gospel music is that for me."**

John also values his personal relationships, and he draws musical inspiration from loved ones. He is currently single, although he has been linked to some glamorous women in recent years. In 2006, he began dating a beautiful dark-haired Brazilian model named Danielle Abreu. The media speculated that John and Danielle

Since becoming a celebrity, John has dated a number of beautiful women, but has not managed to maintain a long-term relationship. He was briefly linked to Jessica White, a model who appeared in *Sports Illustrated*'s swimsuit issue. In 2006 John began dating Danielle Abreu (pictured here), a Brazilian model, but they had broken up by early 2007.

would become a permanent pair. But by Valentine's Day of 2007, John was single again.

His high-flying career makes sustaining a romantic relationship difficult, though. In 2006, he explained to a reporter that his busy touring schedule leaves little time for long-term commitment:

The future looks bright for John Legend, shown in this photograph taken at a celebrity event in April 2007. That month his North American tour began, with shows in such major cities as San Diego, Denver, Chicago, Boston, New York, Atlanta, and New Orleans. The award-winning English singer Corinne Bailey Rae was John's opening act on the tour.

> **"The music business is the worst one to sustain relationships in, because you're in a different city every day and you have lots of women throwing themselves at you. So you have to be disciplined and be with someone who trusts you—and who you don't want to cheat on."**

What the Future Holds

John may eventually settle down with a special someone. For now, though, he devotes his energy to singing and songwriting. His life has never been busier. The young performer's profile continues to increase as publicity and entertainment requests pour in from companies and charities around the world.

In 2007, John appeared on a television spot with other famous graduates of the University of Pennsylvania. The ad showcased top alumni like John in order to promote the college. John's TV voiceover described the school as a breeding ground for creative genius.

John's life has changed dramatically since he graduated from Penn in 1999 and took his first full-time job with Boston Consulting Group. In a recent *Washington Post* interview, he joked about returning to his old New York office building someday—not to work at BCG, but to perform:

> **"They'd have to pay me more for one show than I made every year there. They're particularly proud of me. They use me in their recruiting brochures."**

John's brief experience in the business world paid a respectable salary, and it also gave him useful skills for his music career. At BCG, he learned about finance, marketing, and making deals. In recent years he has signed lucrative deals with HBO, J.C. Penney, Starbucks, Target, Verizon, and Baileys. All of these companies have agreed to help promote his music.

In the New York offices of BCG, none of the people who worked with John could have predicted that the polite, studious boy from Ohio would rise to become an international recording star only a few years later. And yet today John Legend is truly a legend in the making. With eleven Grammy nominations and five award wins, the young artist appears to be living up to his name.

1978 John Stephens is born on December 28 in Springfield, Ohio.

1995 Graduates as the salutatorian of Springfield North High School in Ohio.

1998 Plays the piano on Lauryn Hill's hit album *The Miseducation of Lauryn Hill.*

1999 Graduates magna cum laude from the University of Pennsylvania, majoring in English. He takes a job with the Boston Consulting Group and moves to New York City.

2000 John produces and releases his first CD, *John Stephens,* which he sells to fans at his shows and through his Web site.

2001 John's former college roommate, Devo Springsteen, introduces him to his cousin, an up-and-coming music producer named Kanye West, in New York City.

John's second self-produced CD, *Live at Jimmy's Uptown,* is released.

2002 Releases a third self-produced CD, *Live at SOBs.*

2003 Releases a fourth self-produced CD, *Solo Sessions Vol. 1: Live at the Knitting Factory.*

2004 John performs on Kanye's debut album, *The College Dropout.*

He signs a contract with Columbia Records.

During the summer he tours with Kanye and Usher.

On his 26th birthday, his first professional album, *Get Lifted,* is released.

2005 John portrays Stevie Wonder in an episode of the television drama *American Dreams.*

He covers Wonder's song "Don't You Worry 'Bout a Thing" for the soundtrack to the movie *Hitch.*

At the BET Awards show on June 28, John plays a duet with Stevie Wonder and he accepts an award for Best New Artist.

2006 John performs before the Super Bowl in Detroit on February 5.

He performs at halftime of the NBA All-Star Game in Houston on February 19.

At the 48th annual Grammy Awards Show in Los Angeles on February 28, he performs "Ordinary People" and wins three Grammy Awards.

He also wins two awards at the Soul Train Music Awards on March 10.

On October 24, his second album, *Once Again*, is released.

2007 Performs with Corinne Bailey Rae and John Mayer at the Grammys, and wins two more Grammy Awards.

On April 21, John performs at the Laureus Foundation's All-Star Celebrity Polo Challenge in Palm Beach, Florida.

ACCOMPLISHMENTS & AWARDS

Awards

2005 Nominated, Best R&B/Soul or Rap New Artist, Soul Train Awards.

Winner, Best New Artist, BET Awards.

Nominated, Best Male R&B Artist, BET Awards.

2006 Winner, Best R&B Male Vocal Performance ("Ordinary People"), Grammy Awards.

Winner, Best R&B Album (*Get Lifted*), Grammy Awards.

Winner, Best New Artist, Grammy Awards.

Nominated, Best Rap/Sung Collaboration ("They Say"), Grammy Awards.

Nominated, Song of the Year ("Ordinary People"), Grammy Awards.

Nominated, Best R&B Song ("Ordinary People"), Grammy Awards.

Nominated, Best Traditional R&B Vocal Performance ("Stay With Me"), Grammy Awards.

Nominated, Best R&B Performance by a Duo or Group ("So High"), Grammy Awards.

Winner, Best R&B/Soul Album Male (*Get Lifted*), Soul Train Awards.

Winner, Best R&B/Soul Single Male ("Ordinary People"), Soul Train Awards.

2007 Winner, Best Male R&B Vocal Performance ("Heaven"), Grammy Awards, 2007

Winner, Best R&B Performance by a Duo or Group ("Family Affair"), Grammy Awards.

Nominated, Best Male Pop Vocal Performance ("Save Room"), Grammy Awards.

Winner, Best R&B/Soul Single Male ("Save Room"), Soul Train Awards.

Nominated, Best R&B/Soul Album Male (*Once Again*), Soul Train Awards.

Periodicals

du Lac, J. Freedom "The Best New Artist is Already a Legend." *The Washington Post*, February 9, 2006.

———. "John Legend, 'Once Again' in His Own Good Time." *The Washington Post*, October 24, 2006.

"John Legend: Singer-Pianist Stirs the Soul and Takes Music to Higher Ground With CD 'Get Lifted.'" *Jet*, March 21, 2005.

Jones, Steve. "Legend, In His Own Time." *USA Today*, February 2, 2006.

Michel, Sia. "Charms of the Not-So-Bad Boy." *The New York Times*, November 1, 2006.

Odell, Jennifer. "John Legend Sounds Off." People vol. 63, no. 11 (March 21, 2005): p. 56.

Scaggs, Austin. "John Legend." Rolling Stone no. 1,012 (November 2, 2006): p. 30–33.

Watson, Margeaux. "John Legend." *Entertainment Weekly*, November 10, 2006.

Web Sites

www.johnlegend.com
John's official Web site includes his biographical information, news about upcoming tours, album information, audio clips, and photos.

www.johnlegendnetwork.com
John's official fan club provides members with exclusive access to ticket giveaways and premier concert seating.

www.john-legend.net
The leading unofficial fan site for John keeps music lovers up-to-date about the star's latest news and media coverage.

www.myspace.com/johnlegend
On his MySpace page, John blogs about music, politics, and his personal life.

www.upenn.edu/gazette/0105/feature03.html
John's college magazine, *The Pennsylvania Gazette*, published an in-depth profile of his rise to fame.

a cappella—a style of musical performance that uses voices without any other instruments.

amateur—done in a way that is not professional.

arrangement—a piece of music rewritten by someone (an arranger) with parts to be played by instruments or voices.

Black Panthers—an African-American political organization that promoted civil rights for blacks in the 1960s and 1970s.

demeanor—a person's behavior or manner.

gangsta rap—a type of hip-hop music in which the lyrics focus on the experiences of some inner-city residents, often glorifying gang involvement, crime, and drug use.

gig—a job for an entertainer, usually performing live.

gospel music—religious music that originated among African-American Christians in the South and combines folk tunes, spirituals, and jazz.

lyrics—the words of a song.

magna cum laude—a Latin phrase meaning "with high honors," used to distinguish the top students in a graduating class.

platinum—a recording industry designation given to an album that sells more than a million copies.

R&B—rhythm and blues, a music genre with origins in African-American culture that combines elements of jazz, blues, and gospel music.

salutatorian—a name given to the student who graduates with the second-highest grades in his or her class.

savvy—highly experienced and knowledgeable; shrewd.

seamstress—a woman who sews fabric for a living.

session musician—a musician who is paid to play or sing on recordings in a studio, but is not a permanent member of a band.

ABOUT THE AUTHOR

Clara Magram is a writer and pianist living in New York City.

Picture Credits

page

2: Sony/BMG/FPS
6: Abaca Press/KRT
9: jmfoxje-41/INFGoff
11: AFP
12: Sony/BMG/FPS
15: Sony/BMG/FPS
16: Sony/BMG/FPS
18: Newswire Photo Service
20: Zuma Press/UPPA
22: Zuma Press
25: Roca John/GAMMA
26: Zuma Press/UPPA
27: AdMedia/Sipa
29: CI/AdMedia
30: G.O.O.D. Music/Sony Urban

32: InterFoto USA/Sipa
34: UPI Newspictures
36: Lionel Hahn/Abaca Press/KRT
38: WireImage Archive
39: Abaca Press/KRT
41: AFP/Getty Images
42: AFP/Getty Images
43: Ai Wire Foto
44: New Millennium Images
47: CI/AdMedia
49: AFP/Getty Images
50: iPhoto
53: WENN Photos
54: Newswire Photo Service

Front cover: Abaca Press/KRT
Back cover: UPI Newspictures